# Get America Singing
## ...Again!

# Get America Singing ...AGAIN!

## A Project of the Music Educators National Conference

ISBN 978-0-7935-6635-8

**HAL•LEONARD™ CORPORATION**

7777 W. BLUEMOUND RD. P.O. BOX 13819 MILWAUKEE, WI 53213

# TABLE OF CONTENTS

# Foreword

If there's a human race still here in the 22nd Century, I believe we'll learn the fun of singing again. To take a lung full of air and push it out with some kind of song is an act of survival, whether you're singing in a shower, a car, a bar, in a chorus, at a birthday party, at a church, or wherever. Try it — you'll live longer.

Of course, it'll be much harder to find songs all folks want to sing together, but that's alright. Little by little, we're learning to like each other's songs and getting less enthusiastic about killing each other. And if there's still a human race here in 100 years, it won't be because of any one big organization, whether a big church or big political party, a big corporation or country, or even a big UN. It will be because of millions upon millions of small organizations: *Save This. Stop That.* We'll disagree on so many things it'll be funny. But we'll agree on a few main points, like:

- it's better to talk than shoot.
- bombs always kill innocent people.
- when words fail (and they will), try sports, arts and food.

And industrialized, polluted, TV-addicted people will learn to sing again. Hooray!

Pete Seeger
Honorary National Chair,
*Get America Singing ... Again!* Campaign

*Pete Seeger's CD, "Pete" is available from:*
*Living Music Records,*
*P.O. Box 72, Litchfield, CT 06759.*

# Introduction

Rachel Carson's landmark book, <u>Silent Spring</u>, raised the specter of a spring where birds, killed off by pesticides, did not sing anymore. Well, today many of us are starting to worry about whether **people** are singing anymore. We meet increasing numbers of adults who call themselves "non-singers," children who enter kindergarten without having experienced family singing, and teenagers who would rather slap on earphones than sing. What is at stake here is not just singing, but the very spirit of community in our towns, our cities, and our nation. But ... something can be done about it, and this book is a response to that need.

In April, 1995, the Music Educators National Conference* (Will Schmid, John Mahlmann) invited representatives of other organizations – Society for the Preservation and Encouragement of Barbershop Quartet Singing in America (Dan Naumann and Gary Stamm), Sweet Adelines International (Sharon Green), American Choral Directors Association (Lynn Whitten), and Chorus America (Doralene Davis) to meet with us to discuss singing in America. After considerable discussion, we decided to launch a campaign to *Get America Singing ... Again!*

The campaign has two main objectives; the first of which is to establish a common song repertoire that "Americans, of all ages, know and can sing." We need some songs that everyone can sing, not just the good old traditional songs, but copyrighted songs also. This book is a result of a year-long process of sifting through lots of great songs. Some of your favorite songs may not be included, but we had to start somewhere, and this is the result. Keith Mardak, president of the Hal Leonard Corporation, then volunteered to help with this project by publishing the books and returning a portion of the cost of each book to the *Get America Singing ... Again!* campaign.

The campaign's second objective is to promote community singing. This includes encouraging audience singing at concerts and recitals, opening or closing public gatherings with a song, and encouraging singing at clubs, private meetings, and in homes. We need singing leadership from Americans in all walks of life ... school and church leaders, club presidents, elected civic leaders, radio and TV personalities, camp and scout leaders, and people who get together socially.

So, why not make your own plans to build up the common life of singing in your community? Plan now to include some audience participation at a concert or other public event. Throw in a song or two at the beginning of a meeting to melt the ice and get communication going. Restore the fun of camp singing next time you gather a group around the fire. Get out the guitar, sit down at the piano, tune up the Autoharp, add a bass, drums, or any other instruments you can lay your hands on, and have a sing-along. Think how you can be a positive agent for change; see how singing can add so much to life together on this planet. People will bless you for including them in the power of active music making through singing.

If you would like to contribute to the *Get America Singing ... Again!* campaign, call the Music Educators National Conference (MENC) at 1-800-336-3768.

All the best,
Will Schmid, President
Music Educators National Conference
(1994-96)

* In 1913, MENC (then called the Music Supervisors National Conference) published its first pamphlet of community songs which led to the widely used collections, *55 Community Songs* and *Twice 55 Community Songs*. MENC was also influential in helping the United States arrive at an official version of the *"Star Spangled Banner."* MENC is a professional association of over 65,000 music teachers dedicated to building up America's musical culture and providing an education in music for every child.

*The youngest participants in a San Francisco Music Week sing "America" at Excelsior Playground, circa 1925. From the collection of the Music Educators National Conference Historical Center, University of Maryland, College Park.*

# Amazing Grace

Words by JOHN NEWTON
Sacred Harp Spiritual

**Moderately**

Lyrics:

maz - ing grace, how sweet the sound that saved a wretch like
grace that taught my heart to fear and grace my fears re-
man - y dan - gers, toils and snares, I have al - read - y

me. I once was lost, but now am found, was
lieved. How pre - cious did that grace ap - pear, the
come. 'Tis grace has brought me safe thus far, and

blind, but now I see. 'Twas
hour I first be - lieved. Through

home.

# America
## (My Country 'Tis of Thee)

Words by SAMUEL FRANCIS SMITH
Music is Traditional

# America the Beautiful

Words by KATHERINE LEE BATES
Music by SAMUEL A. WARD

# Battle Hymn of the Republic

Words by JULIA WARD HOWE
Music by WILLIAM STEFFE

**Spirited March**

Mine

eyes have seen the glo - ry of the com - ing of the Lord. He is tram - pling out the vin - tage where the
sound - ed forth the trum - pet that shall nev - er call re - treat. He is sift - ing out the hearts of men be -

grapes of wrath are stored. He hath loos'd the fate - ful light - ning of His ter - ri - ble swift sword. His
fore His judge - ment seat. O be swift, my soul, to an - swer Him, be ju - bi - lant, my feet. Our

*From BETSY*
# Blue Skies

**Words and Music by IRVING BERLIN**

# Danny Boy
## (Londonderry Air)

Words by FREDERICK EDWARD WEATHERLY
Music is Irish Traditional

there in sun-shine or in shad-ow, oh, Dan-ny Boy, oh Dan-ny Boy, I love you so!

# De colores

Mexican Folk Song

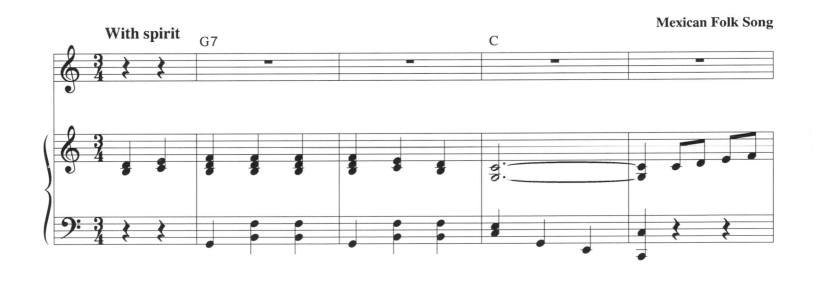

All_____ the col - ors, all the col - ors that
De_____ co - lo - res, de co - lo - res se

*From THE SOUND OF MUSIC*

# Do-Re-Mi

Lyrics by OSCAR HAMMERSTEIN II
Music by RICHARD RODGERS

# Down by the Riverside

African American Spiritual

# Frère Jacques

French Round*

Frè-re Jac-ques, Frè-re Jac-ques, Dor-mez vous,
Are you sleep-ing, are you sleep-ing, Broth-er John,

dor-mez vous? Son-nez les ma-ti-nes, son-nez les ma-ti-nes, Din din don, din din don.
Broth-er John? Morn-ing bells are ring-ing, morn-ing bells are ring-ing, Ding ding dong, ding ding dong.

*May be sung as a round,
with entrances at indicated numbers.

*From GEORGE M!*

# Give My Regards to Broadway

Words and Music by GEORGE M. COHAN

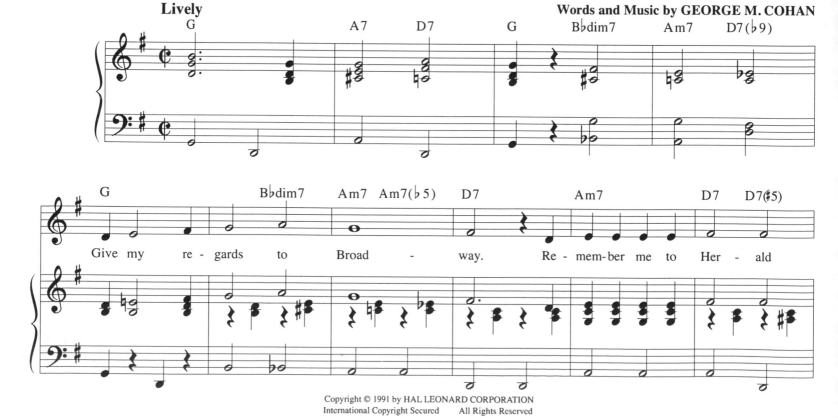

Give my re-gards to Broad - way. Re-mem-ber me to Her - ald

# God Bless America

Words and Music by IRVING BERLIN

# God Bless the U.S.A.

Words and Music by LEE GREENWOOD

And I'm proud to be an A-mer-i-can— where at least I know I'm free. And I won't for-get the men who died, who gave that right to me. And I'd glad-ly stand up, next to you— and de-fend her still to-day. 'Cause there ain't no doubt I love this land,— God bless the U. S. A. From the

MCA music publishing

# Green Green Grass of Home

Words and Music by CURLY PUTMAN

# Havah Nagilah
## (Let Us Rejoice and Be Happy)

Traditional Hebrew

# He's Got the Whole World in His Hands

African American Spiritual

# Home on the Range

**Traditional Cowboy Song**

# I've Been Working on the Railroad

**With Vigor**

**Traditional American Folk Song**

Lyrics:

I've been work-ing on the rail - road, all the live-long day. I've been work-ing on the rail - road, just to pass the time a - way. Can't you hear the whis-tle blow - in'? Rise up so ear-ly in the morn. Can't you hear the cap-tain shout - in', "Di - nah, blow your horn?" Di - nah, won't you blow, Di - nah, won't you blow,

# If I Had a Hammer
## (The Hammer Song)

Words and Music by LEE HAYS
and PETE SEEGER

# Let There Be Peace on Earth

Words and Music by SY MILLER and JILL JACKSON

# Lift Ev'ry Voice and Sing

Music by JAMES WELDON JOHNSON
Music by J. ROSAMOND JOHNSON

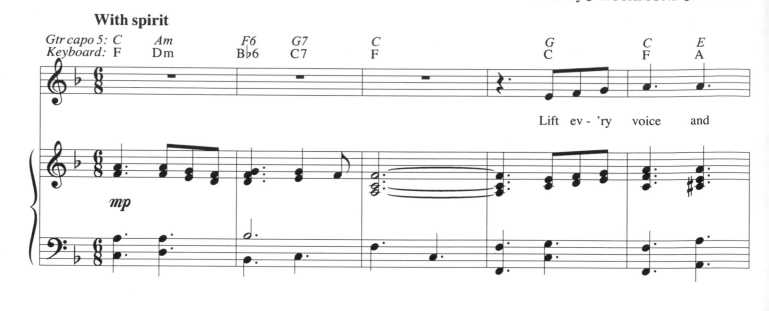

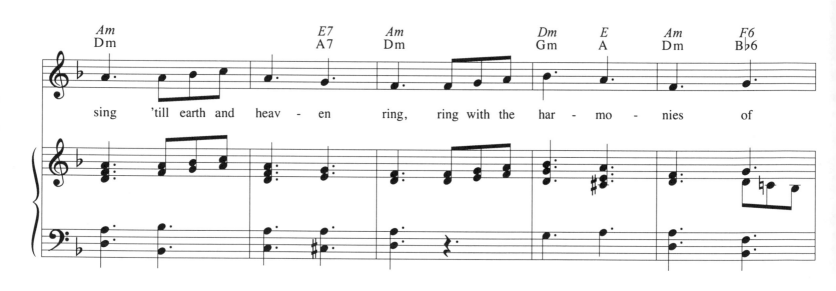

# Michael
## (Row the Boat Ashore)

African American Spiritual

# Dona Nobis Pacem

**Traditional Canon\***

\*May be sung as a round,
with entrances at indicated numbers.

# Music Alone Shall Live

**Traditional***

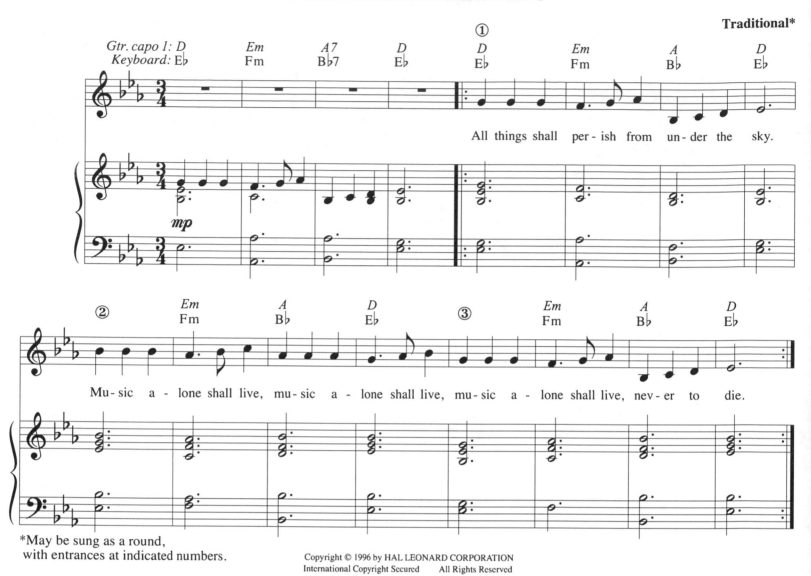

All things shall per-ish from un-der the sky.

Mu-sic a-lone shall live, mu-sic a-lone shall live, mu-sic a-lone shall live, nev-er to die.

*May be sung as a round,
with entrances at indicated numbers.

# My Bonnie Lies Over the Ocean

**Moderate waltz tempo**

**Traditional**

My Bon-nie lies o-ver the o-cean,

*From OKLAHOMA!*

# Oh, What a Beautiful Mornin'

Lyrics by OSCAR HAMMERSTEIN II
Music by RICHARD RODGERS

# Oh! Susanna

**Words and Music by STEPHEN COLLINS FOSTER**

# Over My Head

**African American Spiritual**
**Text adapted for**
**National Arts Standards**

**1, 2, 3** / F  **4** / F

There must be joy some-where._____ In my where._____

# Puff the Magic Dragon

Words by LEONARD LIPTON
Music by PETER YARROW

**Moderately**

Puff, the mag-ic drag-on lived by__ the sea. and frol-icked in__ the
geth-er they would tra-vel on a boat with bil-lowed sail.  Jack-ie kept__ a

au-tumn mist__ in a land called Hon-a-lee.__  Lit-tle Jack-ie Pa-per loved that ras-cal
look-out perched__on Puff's gi-gan-tic tail.__  No-ble kings and prin-ces would bow when-e'er they

# Rock-A-My Soul

African American Spiritual

# Sakura

Japanese Folk Song

Sakura, Sakura, cher-ry blos-soms
*Sa-ku-ra, Sa-ku-ra. Ya-yo-i no*

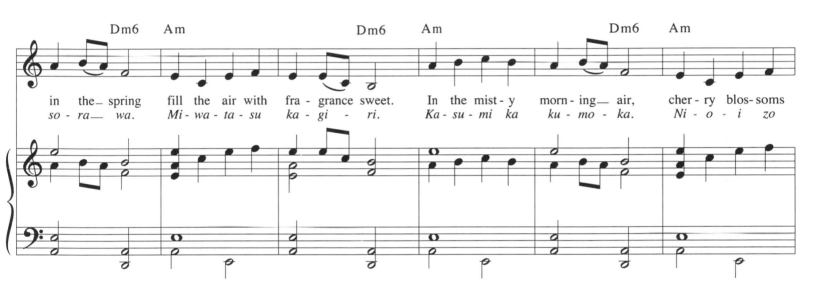

in the spring fill the air with fra-grance sweet. In the mist-y morn-ing air, cher-ry blos-soms
*so-ra wa. Mi-wa-ta-su ka-gi-ri. Ka-su-mi ka ku-mo-ka. Ni-o-i zo*

ev-'ry-where. Sakura, Sakura, cher-ry blos-soms in the spring.
*i-zu-ru: i-za-ya, i-za-ya Mi ni yu-kan.*

# Shalom Chaverim
## (Peace, Friend, Until We Meet Again)

Traditional Hebrew*

Sha - lom cha - ve - rim, sha - lom cha - ve - rim, sha - lom, sha -
lom. L' hit ra — ot, l' hit ra — ot, sha - lom sha - lom.

*May be sung as a round over a
D minor accompaniment

# She'll be Comin' 'Round the Mountain

Traditional

She'll be com - in' 'round the
driv - in' six white
all go out to

# Shenandoah

**Traditional Sea Chantey**

Oh, Shen-an-doah,⸺ I long to hear you.
Shen-an-doah,⸺ I'm bound to leave you.
A-

way⸺ you roll-ing riv-er.
Oh, Shen-an-doah,⸺ I long to hear you.
Oh, Shen-an-doah,⸺ I'll not de-ceive you.
A-

way,⸺ I'm bound a-way, 'cross the wide⸺ Mis-sour - i. Oh, i.

# Simple Gifts

**Traditional Shaker Hymn**

# Sometimes I Feel Like a Motherless Child

**African American Spiritual**

Some-times I feel like a moth-er-less child, some-times I feel like a moth-er-less child. Some-times I feel like a moth-er-less child, a might-y long way— from home.— Yes, a long, long way— from home. True be-liev-er, I'm a long, long way— from home,— yes, a long, long way— from home.

# Swing Low, Sweet Chariot

**African American Spiritual**

home.    Swing low, sweet char - i - ot,____ com-in' for to car-ry me home.

Swing_ low, sweet char - i - ot,____ com-in' for to car-ry me home.

# This Land Is Your Land

Words and Music by WOODY GUTHRIE

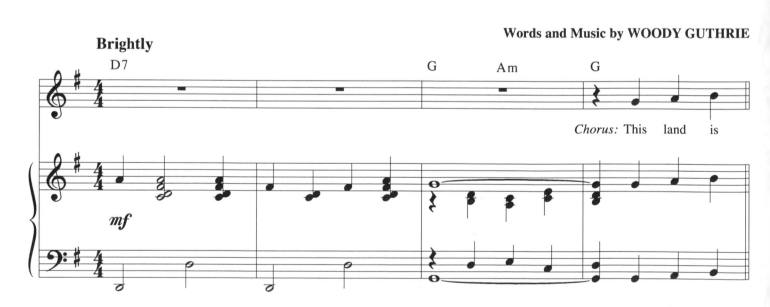

*Chorus:* This    land    is

# Take Me Out to the Ball Game

Words by JACK NORWORTH
Music by ALBERT von TILZER

# The Star Spangled Banner

Words by FRANCIS SCOTT KEY
Music by JOHN STAFFORD SMITH

# Yesterday

Words and Music by JOHN LENNON
and PAUL McCARTNEY

**Moderately, with expression**

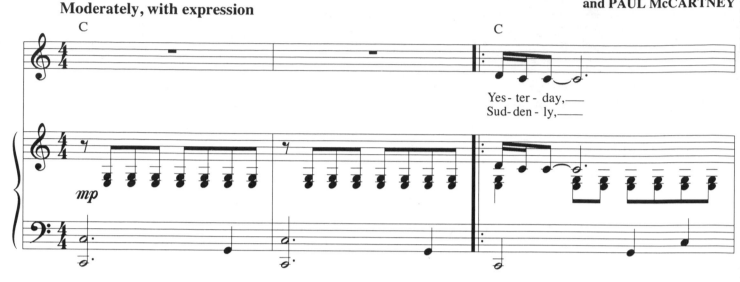

Yes- ter - day,___
Sud- den- ly,___

all my trou- bles seemed so far a - way.___ Now it looks as though they're
I'm not half the man_ I used to be.___ There's a shad- ow hang - ing

here to stay,___ oh I be- lieve___ in yes - ter - day.___
o - ver me,___ oh yes - ter - day___ came sud- den - ly.___

*From Walt Disney's SONG OF THE SOUTH*

# Zip-A-Dee-Doo-Dah

**Words by RAY GILBERT**
**Music by ALLIE WRUBEL**

# This Little Light of Mine

African American Spiritual